You Little Monkey!

and other poems
for young children

by John Foster

Illustrated by
Jan Lewis

Oxford University Press

Oxford   New York   Toronto

OXFORD
UNIVERSITY PRESS
Great Clarendon Street, Oxford OX2 6DP

Oxford University Press is a department of the University of Oxford.
It furthers the University's objective of excellence in research, scholarship,
and education by publishing worldwide in

Oxford New York

Athens Auckland Bangkok Bogotá Buenos Aires
Cape Town Chennai Dar es Salaam Delhi Florence Hong Kong Istanbul
Karachi Kolkata Kuala Lumpur Madrid Melbourne Mexico City Mumbai
Nairobi Paris São Paulo Shanghai Singapore Taipei Tokyo Toronto Warsaw

with associated companies in Berlin Ibadan

Oxford is a registered trade mark of Oxford University Press
in the UK and in certain other countries

Text Copyright © John Foster 1996
Illustrations Copyright © Jan Lewis 1996
First published 1996
First published in this edition 2002
The moral rights of the author/artist have been asserted

Database right Oxford University Press (maker)

British Library Cataloguing in Publication Data available

ISBN 0 19 276259 1

1 3 5 7 9 10 8 6 4 2

Printed in China

CONTENTS

This morning my dad shouted

This morning my dad shouted.
This morning my dad swore.
There was water through the ceiling.
There was water on the floor.
There was water on the carpets.
There was water down the stairs.
The kitchen stools were floating
So were the dining chairs.

This morning I've been crying.
Dad made me so upset.
He shouted and he swore at me
Just 'cause things got so wet.
I only turned the tap on
To get myself a drink.
The trouble is I didn't see
The plug was in the sink.

There's a hole in my pants

There's a hole in my pants.
It's our washing machine.
It's eating our clothes,
Not washing them clean.

As it churns round and round,
It snorts and it snickers,
Chewing holes in Dad's shirts
And shredding Mum's knickers.

It's swallowed a sock.
We can't open the door.
It's bubbling out soap suds
All over the floor.

There's a monster that lives
In our washing machine.
It's eating our clothes,
Not washing them clean.

The shirts on the line

On a windy day
The shirts on the line
Wave their arms about
Dancing up and down.

On a sunny day
The shirts on the line
Stretch out
And sunbathe.

On a frosty day
The shirts on the line
Shiver and freeze
As stiff as statues.

On breezy days
The shirts on the line
Flap their arms
And whisper in the wind.

When the wind blows

When the wind blows
Clouds charge across the sky
Like huge white balloons
Which have snapped their strings.

When the wind blows
Leaves scuttle across pavements
And cluster in corners
As if they are frightened.

When the wind blows
Hats escape from heads
And scamper down the street
Like naughty children.

When the wind blows
Crisp packets play kiss-chase
Then flatten themselves
Exhausted against the playground fence.

My look-out tower

The climbing-frame
In our garden
Is my look-out tower.
From the top you can see
Over next door's hedge
To the road beyond.

Every evening in summer
I take the first watch
From half-past five to six,
While Dad patrols the kitchen
Getting the tea ready.

When I see our car,
I signal to Dad,
Then scramble down
As fast as I can.

That's why
When Mum comes in
Her tea's always ready.

That's why
When Mum comes in
I'm always ready
To give her a hug.

Smugglers

This morning,
While Mum was having a lie-in,
Because it's Saturday,
My sister and I
Emptied our money-boxes
And went down town
To buy the scarf
We know she'll like.

When we got home,
My sister went in first
And kept her talking,
While I smuggled the scarf upstairs
And hid it in the shoe-box
Under my bed.

This afternoon,
We'll go down to the flower shop with Dad
And we'll smuggle a plant
Into the shed.

Tonight,
We'll write the cards
We smuggled in
Earlier in the week
And wrap up the scarf.

Then, in the morning,
We'll give ourselves up,
Hand over the smuggled goods
And watch Mum's face
As she opens her presents
On Mother's Day.

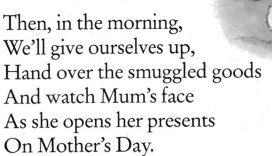

Grandma

Grandma is navy blue.
She is a comfy cushion.
Grandma is a soft whisper.
She is a path through a winter wood.
Grandma is a warm scarf.
She is a cup of tea by the fire.
Grandma is a sleeping cat.
She is autumn sunshine.

The library lady

The library lady
Has grey hair
Like Grandma's.
She never gets cross.
Once I spilled
Orange juice
All over the cover
Of my book.
When I told her,
She just said,
'Never mind.
Try not to do it again.'
When I was ill,
I was late
Taking my books back.
She just said,
'Where were you last week?
I missed you.
Are you better now?'

The library lady
Helps me to find
The books I like.
She knows
All the exciting stories
And the scary ones.

When I grow up
I'd like to work
In a library.

11

At the school for young dragons

At the school for young dragons
The main lessons are
Flying and feasting and fighting.

In flying they learn
How to take off and land
How to dive and to swoop
How to loop the loop
And how to leave trails of sky-writing.

In feasting they learn
About how to behave
When invited to dine
In an old dragon's cave.
They learn that it's rude
To gobble your food,
That you should not belch fire
That you must always sit up straight
And never, ever, scorch your plate.

In fighting they learn
How to scare off their foes
With jets of flame
That will singe their toes,
How to puff a smoke screen
So they cannot be seen.
How a knight with a lance
Hasn't much of a chance
Against dragons who know
How a whack of the tail
Can shatter chain-mail.

At the school for young dragons
The main lessons are
Flying and feasting and fighting,
Which is why you will hear
A young dragon say,
'Our lessons are really exciting!
It's better than reading and writing!'

13

I'm painting a picture

I'm painting a picture of a dragon
With claws as sharp as nails
With bright red eyes
A pointed tail
And shining silver scales.

I'm painting a picture of a wizard
With a pointed hat on his head,
Reading a book
Of magic spells
And eating his breakfast in bed.

I'm painting a picture of a ghost
Standing behind a door,
Holding a chain
That rattles and clanks
When he drags it across the floor.

I'm painting a picture of a giant
Sitting and washing his hair,
Having a bath
In the castle moat
Blowing soap bubbles in the air.

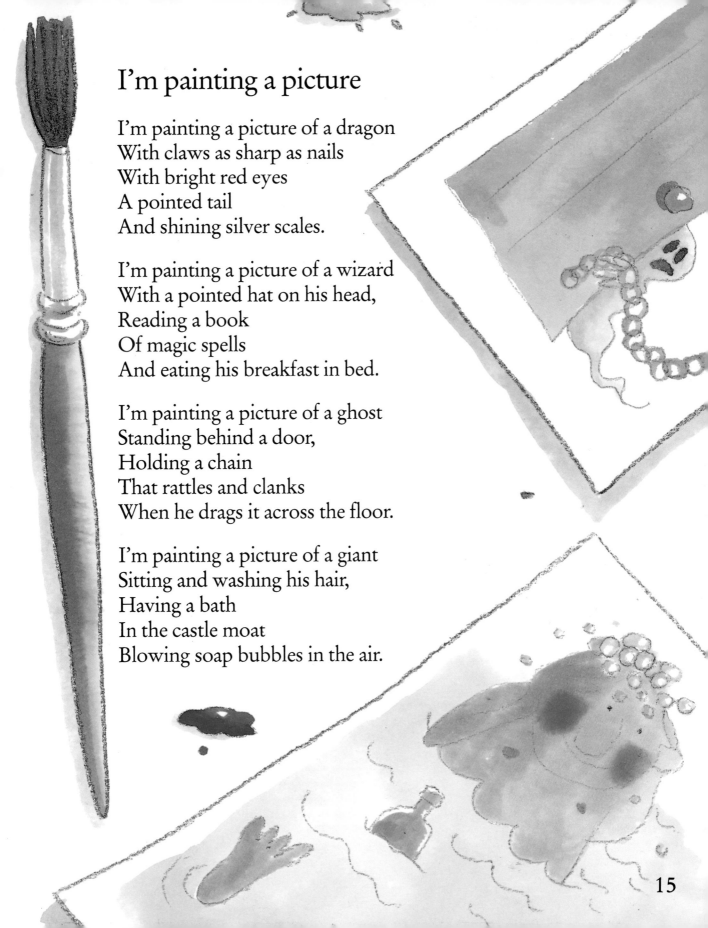

Night-time, Fright time

Night-time, fright time,
Please leave on the light time.

Night-time. Shadows creep.
Floorboards creak. Can't sleep.

Night-time, fright time,
Please leave on the light time.

Night-time. Darkness hides.
Goblin chuckles. Ghost glides.

Night time, fright time,
Please leave on the light time.

Night-time, fear time,
Something's creeping near time.

Night-time, fright time,
PLEASE LEAVE ON THE LIGHT TIME!

What's that?

What's that rustling at the window?
Only the curtain flapping in the breeze.

What's that groaning in the garden?
Only the branches swaying in the trees.

What's that rattling at the front door?
Only the wind in the letter-box flap.

What's that drumming in the bathroom?
Only the dripping of the leaking tap.

What's that hissing in the front room?
Only the gas as it burns in the fire.

What's that murmur in the kitchen?
Only the whirring of the tumble drier.

What's that shadow lurking
  in the corner beside the door?
It's only your clothes where you left them
  lying on the bedroom floor.

Who's afraid?

Do I have to go haunting tonight?
The children might give me a fright.
It's dark in that house.
I might meet a mouse.
Do I have to go haunting tonight?

I don't like the way they scream out,
When they see me drifting about.
I'd much rather stay here,
Where there's nothing to fear.
Do I have to go haunting tonight?

Waking at Gran's

Sometimes,
When I stay at Gran's,
I wake up in the morning
And can't remember
Where I am.

I feel a moment's fear
That overnight
Someone has changed
The colour of the curtains,
Re-papered the walls
And moved the door of the bedroom.

Then I hear Gran
Moving about downstairs,
Chattering to the budgie,
As she makes my breakfast.

At once,
The world snaps into focus:
I know where I am
And that last night
I slept in the bedroom at Gran's
Where Mum used to sleep
When she was little
And my fear
Disappears.

Overnight

Overnight,
While we slept,
The snow crept
Out of the sky
And blew its white breath
Over doorsteps and sills,
Gardens, fields, and hills.
We woke to find
A world turned white
Overnight.

Ten white snowmen

Ten white snowmen standing in a line,
One toppled over, then there were nine.

Nine white snowmen standing up straight,
One lost his balance, then there were eight.

Eight white snowmen in a snowy heaven,
The wind blew one over, then there were seven.

Seven white snowmen with pipes made of sticks,
One slumped to the ground, then there were six.

Six white snowmen standing by the drive,
One got knocked down, then there were five.

Five white snowmen outside the front door,
An icicle fell on one, then there were four.

Four white snowmen standing by the tree,
One slipped and fell apart, then there were three.

Three white snowmen underneath the yew,
One crumbled overnight, then there were two.

Two white snowmen standing in the sun,
One melted right down, then there was one.

One white snowman standing all alone,
Vanished without a trace, then there was none.

The brown bear

In winter,
When the cold winds blow,
When the land
Is covered with snow,
The brown bear sleeps.

In winter,
When the nights come soon,
When the land
Freezes beneath the moon,
The brown bear dreams.

The brown bear
Dreams of summer heat,
Of berries,
Honey and nuts to eat.
The brown bear sighs.

The brown bear
Stirs, then digs down deep,
Safe and sound
In its winter sleep.
The brown bear dreams.

Magic horse

Black horse,
Magic horse,
Carry me away,
Over the river,
Across the bay
To the sandy beach
Where I can play.

Black horse,
Magic horse,
Carry me away,
Over the seas
To the forest trees
Where I can watch
The tiger cubs play.

Black horse,
Magic horse,
Carry me away
To Arctic snows
Where the cold wind blows
Where I can watch
The polar bears play.

Black horse,
Magic horse,
Carry me away
To golden sands
In far-away lands
Where the sea is blue
And I can play all day.

My zebra

When I go to the shops
I walk down the road
And stop at the place
Where the zebra is lying
Flat on its back
In the middle of the road
Opposite the newsagent's.

When I step carefully
On to its back
All the traffic stops
And the zebra carries me safely
Across the road.

When I've done my shopping
It's still there
Waiting to carry me safely
Back across the road again.

I don't know how
I'd cross the road
Without my zebra.

My shadow

On sunny days
My shadow
Strides ahead of me
Down the street
Or stretches itself out
Behind me
Sticking to my feet.

No matter how hard I try
To shake it off
By going indoors
Or resting in the shade,
It's always there waiting for me
When I come out again.
I've tried to give it the slip
By diving in the swimming-pool,
But when I get out
It's still there,
Standing behind me
Towelling itself dry.

The Mirror Man

The Mirror Man
Knows how I feel.

When I am excited,
His eyes light up.
When I am pleased,
He smiles.
When I am happy,
He laughs.

The Mirror Man
Knows how I feel.

When I am cross,
He scowls.
When I am puzzled,
He frowns.
When I am upset,
He cries.

The Mirror Man
Knows how I feel.

When there is something
I want to keep to myself,
I tell the Mirror Man.
I know my secret
Is safe with him.

Just when

Just when
I was about to fit
the last piece
into the jigsaw,
my baby sister
grabbed my arm
and swept all the pieces
off the table
on to the floor.

That's why,
while they are down there,
having their tea,
I am up here
crying.

27

Brothers and sisters

I've got a sister,
Her name is Amanda.
She's sly and sneaky.
I can't stand her.

I've got a brother,
His name is Ganesh.
I'm sick of the sight of him,
I wish he'd vanish.

I've got a sister.
Her name's Razia.
I'd like to push her
Off the end of a pier.

I've got a brother,
His name is Pete.
He's got hairy legs
And smelly feet.

You little monkey!

My mum said
I was behaving
like a little monkey.

So I climbed
on to the sofa
and started swinging
on the door.

When she told me to stop,
I made chattering noises
and pretended
to scratch my armpits.

I refused
to talk properly
until tea-time,
when all I got
was a plate of nuts
and a banana!

So I decided
to stop
monkeying about.

Sitting in my bath-tub

Sitting in my bath-tub,
I have sailed the seven seas.
I have anchored by the taps.
I've been shipwrecked off the knees.

I have sailed into the unknown
To beat off an attack
From a fleet of pirates lurking
Round behind my back.

I have sailed between the fingers
Where no other ship has been.
I've explored the murky depths
In a soapy submarine.

Sitting in my bath-tub,
I have sailed the seven seas.
I have anchored by the taps.
I've been shipwrecked off the knees.

31

Pretending

I swing on the swing and I fly up high.
I am a brave spaceman exploring the sky.

I stand on my bed and I jump up and down.
I tumble and fall. I'm a circus clown.

I sit in my bath and I play with my ship.
There are rocks and sharks. It's a dangerous trip.

I lie in my bed and I close my eyes tight.
I'm a sailor asleep on the ship of the night.